EMOTIONAL TIME-LAPSE

Poetry, prose, and Who really knows

KATELYNN CHARRON

ISBN: 9798595607100

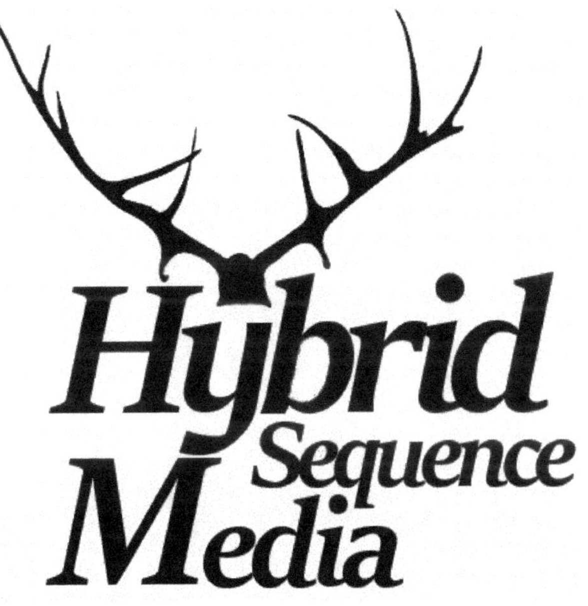

Massachusetts – California
0012

Contents

Emotional Time-Lapse

Poetry, prose, and Who really knows.

Katelynn Charron

Introduction
A call to Expression

This book is a compilation of writings I've done since around 2001. As I work on my other pieces and side projects of children's books, I realized I would like to have something solid in my hands to feel the progress I've been making over the years. To see how far I've come emotionally. (And so, I can get rid of old journals)

It is a, mostly chronological, mix of depression fed writings to positivity fed writings. Hence the title Emotional Time-Lapse. It is written evidence of a process of emotional healing. As a young human I struggled fiercely with self-absorbed depressive thoughts of life and suicide. I found writing to be a wonderful catharsis for this mental scrimmage. Most of the expression here is on the positive side because the more I healed the better I got at expressing myself. There is definitely a good bit here I could find embarrassing, but sometimes being human *is* embarrassing. I refuse to hide it. There is grace in letting people see you fall on your face.

From poetry, prose, to journal entries and back again. Writing these things helped me work through my own shit. I find expression to be a human obligation and a necessity for healing. We all have our unique forms that come naturally to us. This is one of mine. So, if you're here and reading this with me, thank you for this connection you've helped create by picking up this book.

Interaction influenced by heartfelt expression saves lives. Self-expression saves lives. Both the lives of the expressor and those feeling the expressed.

It's an impressive thing being a writer. So much of my life is documented in verbiage. It's like putting pins in flowing emotions and tacking them to a board for later use and embarrassment.

The mind changes, whereas writing does not.
If we allow ourselves to be wrong, we can grow.

So, bear with me through the painful, angsty, adolescent beginning. It picks up pace and goes down again.

**Things dealt with
but not necessarily specifically addressed in this:**
High School and Hormones, moving away from home, Death/Suicide, Father's 16-year battle with cancer, Mothers lifelong struggle with mental illness, Siblings (being the youngest), and your average case of seasonal depression.

Thanks for joining. I hope this moves things around in your brain in a helpful way.

All the love,
-Katelynn
aka Kateland or Katthing

<u>High School & Hormones</u>

(2 Entries from my depressive high school days.)

Class of 2005

<u>24 November 2001</u>

(*14 years old, Attleboro, MA*)

Hello,

My name is Katelynn Jean Charron and I'm not really sure who I am, but I'd like to know. I'm so tired though, I don't even want to keep finding out stuff about myself. I'm tired of getting up in the morning and doing the same thing every day and I'm tired of everyone telling me the same thing. I'd like something different.

<u>**Sometime in 2003**</u>
Session Hall/Detention: I was late to school a lot
(16 years old, Attleboro HS)
School anxiety and depression

All these people kill my brain, when they walk by, I get overwhelmed with this miserable anxiousness. My heart sinks into my stomach. I feel cornered and trapped in my own body. My limbs are tired and weak, my head is throbbing and it's still Monday.

I want this part of me to die. This terribly weak part that makes tears seep from my aching heart. Now my lungs are filling with water and I'm slowly starting to lose grip. I want to let go but I fight until my body falls asleep. My mind wakes in a forest of questions that no one can really answer I feel helpless, hopeless, lonely and lost.

I just want some peace a place of serenity where I can lay my head and smile but all I have are tears.

Where is my happiness? Where is my smile?

<u>The Broken Hearts Head to Ohio</u>

Some context: At almost 19 years old I ended an immature and toxic relationship of 2.5 years. I started a new relationship, in October 2006, with an interesting, wounded, smart, melancholy, self-proclaimed hopeless romantic, that lasted for near 8 years. He's 11.5 years old than I. We moved to Ohio together and lived there from 2008-2010, at his father's house. By this time my own father had had cancer for over 10 years and my emotions were not the most understandable by myself nor my partner.

<u>September 2006</u>
(19 years old)

This maze goes on forever
nothing but dead ends and one-ways
-I'm stuck-
Someone give me a map
or a boost over one of these walls
my heart is screaming for freedom
but my legs won't budge
-Help-
I feel like a fish
sucking in the dry air
that I know will end my life

. . .

<u>**9 May 2008**</u>
(20 years old)

I get so nervous
knowing the newness has faded
plunging forward
just pulling one
and hoping to fly
a unit,
apart from all

we're a brilliant ball of light
running in the darkness

....

I feel my being reach out to you. Fibers so bright you must shade your eyes. Wild, they flail through the air toward you, but they seem to be dancing to the most beautiful music. I feel your breath, the rhythmic beat of your tired heart. It cries like a child. It wants to be put to rest, but I heal you. I heal your aching heart with all of the love in my soul.

. . .

<u>**13 May 2008**</u>
(Ney, Ohio)

The days go by in waves. Some go so fast I'm left confused as to where they went. Some go so slow I'm afraid they'll never end. I wish I felt warmer. The sun's hot but the wind won't stop blowing over these ridiculous flat lands.

. . .

<u>**16 May 2008**</u>
(20 years old. Ney, OH)

I feel a bit better today. It's getting nicer outside. I need the
sunshine.
My heart is like a bomb that constantly explodes.
Thoughts of past fill my head.
High school...
What if I we never broke up... 9th grade... My fickle heart
changes everything.
And now here I am, so in love. Just hoping I'm enough to keep
him happy. He's so in love with everyone he's ever loved.
Makes it hard. Like competition even though I know I'm
already on top...
Hearts a plenty...

. . .

<u>**12 October 2008**</u>
(21 years old, Ney OH)
I don't know if it's just this week or I'm losing it... The pages
just keep turning. Pushing on towards the end, but what's the
story?
Lost in the woods. Losing all hope and faith. Tumbling towards
nothing.

I don't want to lose faith in myself.
I don't want to see just a stupid girl with
a dream
Just a dream
Always thought I saw something better for myself. Hoped I
could be <u>one</u>.
Saw more for my life than just living it.
Giving it, because I had.
Making a difference for being a different.
Because I deserve it.
Because I would do good.
One day.

<u>**December? 2008**</u> blurb
(21 years old)

    Miss everything I'm use to. Everything I'm used to not being use to.
    I'm being used too.

. . .

<u>10 December 2008</u>

    I don't know what future I see. Things always seem to change.
    So much happens to move you. Why can't things just stay the same? Walking down a road with much more path to pass. Praying it's not as rough as the ones that slipped right passed.

Open up my hands. Going with the flow.
Just catch it as it comes and let these pieces fall together,
or apart, as they may.
They'll all find a way.

. . .

and what shall we do now Bacon fang?

<u>**10 August 2009**</u>
(*22 years old*)

I'm digging a hole with a rotted stick
and it keeps breaking...

Sometimes I can see myself snap.
Ripping my own hair out.
Kicking a hole in the wall
Smashing things.
Because, I'm exhausted.
But, because I can look ahead at it, I can see it does no good.
Just hold it all back.
Then it only comes out here and there.

I can feel it... I'm cracking.

. . .

<u>**13 August 2009**</u>

Days have been dragging.
And oh, so lonely.

I'm starting to <u>**hate.**</u>
I feel so angry and no one to talk to.
It makes me nervous and sad
Pushing me over my limit
I hate it here.
Because it's not there.
Because no one is here.
I need help!
Anytime I'm sad he gets angry
How do I talk to him?
I just want to sleep the days away.

. . .

<u>**2009**</u>

Like that first summer day, on your skin, in your lungs.
Waiting. You've been waiting for it. For that light that shines
down deep into your soul – and that warm breeze that caresses
your skin, like small kisses strategically place in all the right
spots...
Just for me, this beautiful day. Just for me.

(same page)
(Ney, OH)

It never seems to be quiet here
This creaky fan constantly going
and the never ending traffic
When all I want all I'd like Is to hear
the fire...
fire
crackling in all it's beautiful glory
speaking its own strange language

I strain my ears to hear,
hear its beautiful words

I hope that it knows I'm listening
and that I cherish it so
because even when it burns to a flicker
I will still watch it glow

. . .

The Freefall of a Teenager in her Twenties

Context: By 2010, 2 years of monotony in Ohio had helped drain us of our shared excitement. The newness of our relationship had faded. My elderly 'married' life at 21 of work all day, home for jeopardy or M*A*S*H, and then bed, was a great and interesting experience and all but, after just over 3 years together, we broke up. Then in March, I headed back to Massachusetts for my father's next inevitable cancer surgery. My partner refused to go back to where we were from so, still in love, we ended things and pushed forward in separate directions. I was incredibly confused. There was an internal chaos that I did not know how to address or vocalize. As you can see, March is hardly dated and there is no April... I was a bit of a mess.

7 January 2010
(Ney, OH. 22 years old)

So, this is the new year
and I feel vastly different.
I almost feel like a new person
with all these new things.

Shiny and new.
No longer waiting.
Pushing ahead on my own
it is so exciting.

The snow keeps falling on these flat lands.
Bitter, white.
That sunshine is calling
It does not go unheard.

This heart feels undone
with no sadness
small fear
big smiles.

Send a question into the wind

−Place your past into a book
Burn the pages let 'em cook

. . .

<u>8 January 2010</u>
(Ney, OH)

Hearts with slippery fingers
spiraling around with top hats
Mad
Looney

Trees frozen to this wintered earth
Crackling fire
The chirps of birds getting farther away

. . .

<u>Assorted March 2010</u>
(South Attleboro/Attleboro MA, 22 years old)

Running in circles, chasing tails
never ending...

Speed dial mind over matter. Continual mind-fuck of beastly proportions. Constipated hearts need cracked skulls. Push, push, pull me under. Move to the beat of that drum, drum, drummer.

Can't hardly wait. Capsizing one another, another one with the ocean, like, 'you're dead to me' only to find you float under the surface because we all float down here. And words just flow on out like endless rain into a paper cup, keeping me and this pen company...

While we drift into the nonsense rat, rat rattling around in there.

. . .

A smoke fight.
Burning embers
and a lingering love.

. . .

The rain falls on the window and dampens my cheeks

. . .

My head spins as the thoughts suffocate me
dizzying
Reaching out to grasp **something**
anything... that's willing
So tired of this weight
This pressure
FIGHTING
Fall back to old roads?
Push on with new goals.
I've lost my balance
Fall fall falling?

. . .

Everything's the same
going through every day

like the last one doesn't matter
wasting all away

everyday

Possibly losing it all
halfway
like a pin prick
Hold still, don't float away

broken train tracks
and delayed planes

you can only take yourself so far
before you have to push

through the door

through the door
nothing left to pour
Just empty and dried up

don't let it happen
don't let it fall

clouded vision
boggled brain
with things that I can't say

duct tape or cotton
my mouth gets in the way

. . .

<u>18 May 2010</u>
(1:30am)

Magic words you'll never hear. Train stations headed nowhere, in the hopes of just, not falling down. Smoke scrapes the sky and makes these bright scars in my mind. I fall back and adjust. Here I am again. Back on these feet. Pulled back on these tracks, and away, not to speak...

Clustered. Battered and bruised, beaten, and kicked down, torn without a thread for stitch or a thought to fill the gap. Emptiness flowing out like oxygen off of leaves. Hopped that train yesterday with tricks up my sleeve.

I think of this skin. Foreign and mysterious. Bright like sunsets unseen. Every inch breathing into me. Gravity pulls me in. It's a science. That blinding light, a sparkle in your eye. That half smile. Chemicals mix and for beauty untouchable. Dangerous, such a form. Tied together. Lost in a tenacious whirlwind.

Dancing with a light heart and a forward march.

. . .

<u>7 June 2010</u>

Why is it I can't be alone with myself without being gone? These thoughts are anchored like feet in cement. Rooted, re-rooted and rooted again...

Thick and pasted to the walls.

Of this head high in the clouds no one knows...

Not even me.

. . .

6 June 2011
12:00
MARCC

Learning to Adapt

Context: At the end of 2010, after 9 months apart, many superficial connections and unaddressed depression, my partner and I got back together. Knowing nothing better than our connection, the logical decision was to try and make it work. He moved back to Massachusetts and we made it through about another 4 years together.

On June 6th 2011, My father has his 6th and final cancer surgery. My stepmother and I go with him and experience some of the most difficult emotions humans have to face. A 15 hour surgery, by the hands of the amazing Samuel Singer at Memorial Sloan Kettering in New York, buys my father 5 more months of life... they expected maybe 2. He lived to see his 48th birthday on September 25th and passed quietly, at home on hospice, with my stepmother and I by his side, on the evening of November 5th 2011.

A person in a state of grief is a different kind of person. It can change you and your relationships. My best friend and I also had a falling out within that period of my depression. Things were not going easy within.

19 April 2011
(146 Union St. Attleboro MA. 23 years old.)

I've felt a heavy fog over my head lately. Maybe it's a mix of things. I should be okay, I think. New house, new life. I'll figure it out I guess... No best friend. Hurts.

My love is always right. His choice usually wins. It's hard on me. Never understands me anymore... I'm scared to talk to him about it because he gets irritated and angry and there's no talking to him then. I don't speak and then eventually I'll explode and let it all out and I'll be so irritated; I won't give a shit if it irritates him.

I'm obviously not too happy about things. I just figure it'll work out. We love each other. Everything will be just fine.

Can't feel these branches reaching
Feeling more like a little shrub
I need more room to grow
Boxed in by a strong love
I feel smaller and smaller
When I know how big I am
Can't let people push me down
Make me feel smaller than I am

. . .

<u>31 May 2011</u>

(23 years old. Helmsly Medical Towers, NYC)

First night in NY. Already feel exhaustion creeping in. This night's love feels cold at the moment. Am I really ready for this? … I'm scared. I feel very alone. Can't seem to put much into words right now. It's as if my thoughts are being strangled. Can't move from brain to hand...

We'll just break it off.

. . .

<u>**26 July 2011**</u>
(24 years old. Attleboro, Massachusetts)

Geez. What do I feel?

Boxed in for sure. Trapped. Stuck. Like I'm not free in my own life. Is it love? If it is what do I do? I wish I had help.
It's like mom just waited until I was 18 so she didn't have to be involved in my life. Now I'm 24 and I'm behind schedule.
What the fuck do I do?
Jump! Up! Onto my own two feet.

The only two feet holding me up.
The only two feet that will ever hold me up.

All I can rely on is me,
but I can't rely on myself
and I don't know why.

I don't know what's holding me back.
I wish I could talk to someone who
could help me.

I feel almost like
I'm incapable of being independent.
Push myself.

I'm all I got.

Don't forget
exit does not exist.

. . .

<u>**17 November 2011**</u>

(24 years old. 12 days after my father died)

There's this large empty space in my head. In the area that is consumed with worry. Most of my life that area was filled with thoughts of my father. Worry. Cancer. Surgery. My life revolved around my father and his illness. He was my best friend.

Now...

I feel like taking off. He told me I couldn't move to Africa. Well, now I can if I want to. I feel like I need to. Need to get out of here. Need to go. Somewhere new. Because this is a new road in my life, a new path in my brain.

I don't want to feel empty.

I miss him so much already and it's still hard to believe he's gone. I won't ever see him again. In this life at least. God, I hope you're right.

I love you Dad. I don't know how I'm supposed to go through life without you being a phone call or a drive away. I can't help but feel like this wasn't supposed to happen to you. And...

<u>**I'm so afraid of forgetting**</u>.

I'm so young. I'm so afraid of forgetting. I don't want to forget his hugs. He told me I was the best hugger. He'd hold me in his arms for minutes. His love. He was such an amazing father. His laugh. God, I loved that laugh. That laugh when he said something inappropriate and he'd put one hand to his mouth and use the other to shoo or slap at you as if you said it, or you made him say it. Or just tap you because you shouldn't be laughing. His jokes… (when I'd yawn) *"Last time I saw a mouth like THAT it had a HOOK in it!"* – or while in the passenger seat of his car, *"One time! I caught a fish this big!* (widens hands, one right in front of your face) *and his tail went like that!"* (proceeds to waggle hand and slap my cheek) – *"Hay is for horses, not for cows! Pigs would eat it but they don't know how!"*, Or the family inside classic *"…* No, wait a minute! That was my cousin!"

God, I'm gonna miss you my whole life. You were the best human I knew. Big heart always worried about us. You were beautiful. And so is your memory. You will stay forever as you were in my heart. And I will never forget how blessed I am just to have had you in my life, never mind getting to call you Dad.

. . .

2012 at some point

Some day, maybe we'll have a baby,
and maybe you'll grow up
while I grow old
hope to be happy and not so stoned

. . .

29 January 2012
(24 years old)

Struggling with this grip on my life.
Like a line all fuzzy
out of focus.

Not so many rocks to stand on.
The waves pull back to sea.
WE STOOD UP WITH OPEN EYES
trying not to see
Honest life frosted over
and burned by all we do

It's there, not it's gone.

no thanks to you and you Proud steps to brighter
future... and you believe it's true
What happened to the voices of peace and sanity?
Dreamers and believers are here to scarcely.

. . .

<u>31 January 2012</u>
(on a plane)

Moving through the fog when time stands still.

Feel feet in concrete.
Brain ticks seconds away counting down the past

and it moves forward,
shifts, and spreads out
like the stars above us.

Every moment is now.

Amazing how 'at one' I feel with life
and earth while in the sky
in something man made.

The beauty that is this earth.
Trees. Every blade of grass.

Every stone.
All so beautiful and also
all so forgotten.

The earth curves for you.
Breathe it in

. . .

<u>15 February 2012</u>
(*146 Union St. Attleboro, MA*)

I love you Dad, It's so hard to believe you're gone from me. I'm definitely not okay with it. But if you truly are in a better place, then I am okay. For you. I have to be.

. . .

<u>1 March 2012</u>
(*Cousin Nicholas's 18th birthday*)

This whole writing thing seems to get harder and harder
as time goes by.
Life is so strange.
Love, Emotions. Stupid.
I want control over my brain.
I want to be able to **DO**.
WRITE! SPEAK! LIVE!
Listening to life go right on by.
I'll be 25 in 4 months. Just a baby.
Really. I know nothing but I sure fucking FEEL.
It's stupid. Strong emotions and a nearly empty head.
The body feels what it feels.
I'm trying to coax it. Meditate on things.
Convince myself. Program myself.
Reason.

I can't wait to go SEE.
Eyes open, mouth closed.
Listen and soak it up.
I need my mind blown.

. . .

<u>**13 March 2012**</u>

So much lost and so much gained
where to lay this ever-expanding brain?

To convince yourself everything is okay,
 hold onto hope another day?

Not holding, squeezing. Suffocating HOPE.
Is it even really there?

. . .

<u>**27 March 2012**</u>

Had a flashback today while I was at work. A scent flashed me back to the hospital hallway in New York... Weird how I'll never experience those feelings again. Amazing how a scent can bring out emotions. Had to **breathe**. Almost started crying...

. . .

<u>**28 March 2012**</u>

So tired of feeling this way.
Totally fucking neglected.
Hurt.
Tired.
Sick.
Annoyed.
Miserable.
Unsatisfied.
Love, laughter...
anything else?

Fuck.

<u>29 March 2012</u>

Keeping this distance is going to damage me.
Damage us,
I know it. I feel it.

'I'm looking through you, where did you go?'
I wonder what's going to happen.
Taken for granted so easily.
'Love has a nasty habit of disappearing overnight...'

. . .

<u>31 March 2012</u>

(8am, Union st, Attleboro, MA)

Growing angry, growing distant.
Growing just to grow.

After all that's broken.
Is this really gonna happen?

. . .

1 April 2012

I've held so much in for so long. I shouldn't have done that. I feel broken and alone. With lack of understanding. From the person who matters most to me.

I watched my father die 5 months ago. How dare you rush my coping. For your sake. How dare you. The person who 'loves' me doesn't understand why losing my father is so hard. I try to tell him, imagine if I died.

No response...

I don't know what I'm supposed to do.

I need you.

I need you to care.

I need you to try.

I want you to understand.

. . .

12 April 2012
(Attleboro, MA)

 Want to get it out. Get it all out.
Get some out? Half out...
Half in...
Words don't flow through this pen like they used to.

 I can have these amazing conversations
but when I stop to think... I... Break.
Broken.

Living this life from the outside.
Someone else is behind the wheel. Him.
He drives this life of mine. It's not fair
and I'm so tired.
Live my life. Even if it pulls me away from him.

Continued later...

The Darkness is over me now. Do you care?
Do you wonder where I am? How it feels?
It's seeping in now, won't take long.
I'll see you on the other side.
But I'll be someone else.
I'll grow to be better. And there you'll be,
lying heartless and a stranger.

Here comes the rain now.
How can you take something for granted twice?

. . .

27 April 2012

Supposed to enjoy the walk.
It's not the destination, it's the path that gets you there.

LIVING on the road to death. I need to push myself.
Slowly but surely.
I need to be assertive.

I'm not okay with myself because I am a procrastinator.
Because I feel jealousy.
Which makes me feel weak and pathetic.
I'm not very independent.

I can be terribly moody for no reason.
Probably because I'm a woman,
but maybe because I'm human.
Learning to understand myself.

. . .

<u>24 May 2012</u>

I've pushed myself to acquire all this stuff inside my head. Filtered peace into my mind by self-awareness. Yet somewhere in some corner up there I know something is not quite right. Like sunshine trying to peak through the darkest rain clouds. Maybe it's fear that keeps this head so cloudy.

Where's the storm that will blow this shit away? Let my eyes see the sun let this heart cry out with joy.

I think I'm on my own way.

. . .

<u>17 August 2012</u>

Head stuck in the clouds.
Feet on the ground?
One foot stuck in the mud.

Stretches thinner than a silk string,
who'd a thought these eyes were so wide.

Who'd a thought at all?
All that thought stretched out in my mind
like a snake of woooooords,
just keeps adding up.

Up to nothing.
Up to a foot in the mud
and reaching for the stars.

. . .

<u>Falling to Rise</u>

Context: My grief and uneasiness in my relationship were at an all-time high by September 2012. I wrote my love a letter expressing my feelings and sat with him while he read it. We decided to work through things, and things were good for a couple months. As time went by, I realized it still wasn't right, I wrote another letter and sat with him while he read it... Him being his sentimental self, kept the last letter I wrote him the year before... Amazingly, *exactly* a year before. SAME DATE a year later. Put them side by side and they about read the same. There was no denying it... Things needed to change.

. . .

<u>6 Sept 2012</u>

Bad dreams fed by my subconscious.
Bad feelings fed by life.
I miss my Dad. His love. His kindness.

I'm just surviving with no stimulation...
I don't even write anymore
My life needs a shove
I can't do this anymore.
I'm wasting days.

I'm tired of surviving... I want to **<u>live</u>**.

. . .

We've built a home around something so hollow.
I thought it was what I wanted
But I think I was just afraid of being alone.
I enjoy being loved.

This sadness is deep in my bones
"I'm sad about so many things"
I miss my father's level head.

. . .

8 Sept 2012

These thoughts are heavy again.
I suppose it's a mix of PMS and things.
Possibly the onset of fall...
I like fall, but it means cold.
And I miss my Dad terribly.
It's such an awful feeling.
Where did my family go?
Where do I go?
What do I do? I'm so lonely.
Life is breathing all around me
and I can't seem to catch my breath.

Something needs to change... obviously things aren't well...

. . .

And The Flowers Follow

I'm seeing the end of the world.
The colors are so bright but I don't want to shade my eyes.
To miss this sight is to die a pointless death.
To fight the pointless fight.

The tears fall, not just for the fallen
but for the beauty of it all...
and I let them.
I find I'm not afraid
The light seeps into my heart
Opening my eyes to sights I've never seen
pulling me into the last moments
like a mother cradling a baby from the cold.
A sweet caress and lifelessness.
Freedom. Peace.
Sleep.
Existence like no one's ever known.
To exist. In that moment
To exist at all.
*<3@
and the flowers follow.

What day is the right day to deal with pain?

. . .

<u>5 October 2012</u>

(6 year Anniversary of our first date)

I am in love with a life.
With a being, a heart.
I am in love with us. But not always.
I'm missing the beauty life has to offer me.
I want to continue to open my mind.

I feel so much pain.
Yours and mine.
Is the best way to just pull away?
I need some proper advice.
My head is everywhere.
I'm constantly hit with second thoughts.
Mostly when I'm tired or high.
But when my head is clear and sober,
I'm so sure.

My heart hurts.
Is this extremely selfish?
It would be wrong to stay. This isn't right.
I hate this.
I may be losing it.
Fighting the urge not to dig into my skin.

. . .

I'm so sorry for the way I feel.
I'm sorry this is happening to us...
I don't think anything I want to say will do any good.
Maybe in time I can say them.
When I'm tired, when I'm high,
I can't even imagine doing this. Going through with this.
I don't know the right way to do this.
I can't make this hurt any less.
I hope you don't hate me.
If you need to. I understand.

I can't help but feel like this is all my doing.
I'm the one making this decision.
And it's hurting both of us.
Life is so strange.
I'm sorry I came into your life and ended up doing this...
You should be happy and smiling.
That's what I want for you.
I'm sorry I feel like it's not with me.
I wish to be your friend all your life.
And I love you.
I'm truly sorry. For all of this.

. . .

<u>8 December 2012</u>

(Union St. couch. Attleboro, MA. 25 years old.)

My mother just called me a bright light in a dimming world. I often feel that way. This world IS so dim. It's so sad. I have hope for people, nonetheless. I miss my father. I miss my brother the way things used to be.

People need to be taught. They need to know that they hold the power and knowledge to make their lives better. To make a difference. To smile. To understand that life is what you make it. That YOU decide to react. YOU choose yourself.
Create yourself. Make yourself. Change yourself. Only you hold the key. Grow. Embrace change. Embrace life, struggle, tears, death. Breathe it all in. There is an amazing beauty to it all. You need to know and believe this in order to find the peace of mind that creates true happiness. Never let go of yourself. Keep a tight grip on your mind. Bend it and stretch it like clay. Stretch it beyond the worlds reach. To the places the give you a mental understanding of life that you can't even describe...
there's a word for that...

Be humbled. When you find peace in yourself you'll see the struggle for it in others. It brings me an overwhelming sense of sadness when I see this struggle. And the ignorance that clouds the mind of a lot of these people. They don't know enough to open their minds beyond it. Beyond EVERYTHING and just BE. And breathe. And look and listen.

The world is alive all around you. And you're missing it all because of the petty things it throws in your way.
Because that's what the people that run all of this want. They need us to be unhappy and uninformed. They need us to care about the media and all the bullshit fed to us. To keep us distracted. To keep us from finding peace, because once you find it, you SEE.

The lies and the insignificance of it all. That's when things get really scary though, but with your mind at peace it's easier to think things through calmly. But where do you start? How do you tell the people of the world they're wasting away? That they're not free. That knowledge is power. That Governments fear their people. As they should.

What push do the people need to take control of their lives? Things we need to teach our children young.

I have so many doubts in life. Doubts about myself, doubts about the world, about people... But I do know if we fed children the proper knowledge to better themselves, to grow and question everything. To know that we are beautiful. To know that life is the most amazing gift, and it shouldn't be wasted feeling sorry for ourselves. That we have no right to feel sorry for ourselves because we get to FEEL at all. If children know this. Then there may be a chance for real life. Real happiness. To be spread and shared. That's important. That's all it takes.
And it's here... on paper.
*<3 @

. . .

<u>Stepping Forward</u>

Context: I changed. He didn't. Instead of growing together, life experience aided in our growing apart. I made a lot of mistakes that I had to learn from. It was painful. We were still in love but knew it wasn't working. In September 2013, after about 7 years of love, we decided to end things. I took a chance and changed my life. Reconnected with an old girlfriend from middle school and moved 3,000 miles away with her to Santa Cruz, California. He followed my lead and ended up in LA. We lingered on romantically for about another year, until we hated each other enough to actually part ways... Thankfully, we are still friends today. Life is strange. I am forever grateful for everything we have shared.

<u>**1 December 2014**</u>
(Santa Cruz, CA. 27 years old)

Love is not possessive.
Did you know that? Real love?
If you **LOVE** someone, how can you want anything besides
<u>their</u> happiness?
NO MATTER WHAT THAT CONSISTS OF
Unconditional love.
I used to feel possessive and jealous.
Ownership...
no
Now, when I love, <u>I</u> feel free.
Love makes me fly.

. . .

I need to tell the world how sad I am.
That I am so happy
I get to feel sad
            and it breaks my heart
and makes me smile
I often think I'd like to feel that for a while.
So, I'm gonna laugh until I cry
and I'm gonna cry until I laugh
and watch this heart break until I die.

Boy, I want to live forever, but I'll sure hug death
when she comes.

If you're not sad, then you're fucked up.

. . .

23 December 2014
(on a bus to LA)

The clouds look lazy laying in these valleys.
White lines fly by my eyes
Someone needs a shower or some clean underwear
Passing through low lying moisture poofs
the fog resembles my overly caffeinated brain.

I think my shit ran off somewhere with my thoughts
guess it's together somewhere else
no surprise to me
wouldn't wanna be my shit either...

. . .

The words don't come like they should
Energy pours from my being
but no adjective or preposition can attempt
to make it make sense
for any of you

They will most certainly say I am mad.
Maybe I am.
Maybe they are
you?
Under a nauseous blanket of ignorance and I'm far too warm
When will the world ever make sense?

I'm merely a light reflection
a speck of star dust
what do you expect from a reflection
of bright cosmic star smut?

. . .

<u>14 April 2015</u>
(27 years old)

This human form is uncomfortable
Being conscious is a blessing as well as a curse.
Being aware of the oneness of all things in the universe yet,
witnessing the tragedy that is human existence.

I'm still learning... and on many occasions
I feel like a tragedy.
When I can see the level, I want for my consciousness
but have to struggle so hard to keep it...

There are boundaries in our minds.
Not often built by ourselves,
though we tend to help support them.
They are learned walls built by other people's perceptions
and how they're taught to us.
Sometimes I can peek over at them
and get a glimpse of the freedom.

Exhausting attempts and I fall back.
All that's left is a memory of a glimpse of what is possible.
Until I have the strength to pull myself up again...
and I will keep in this practice

. . .

14 May 2015

We're not in the same boat.
Nor do our boats look alike.

Do not look at me with the same eyes you use for everyone else.

Do not place upon me you insecure expectations

I like to see these humans as unidentified creatures,
while also putting faith in the psychology of the mind...

Rowing to the same island.
How do you man your boat?

Can you see?

Individualistic cookie cutter

. . .

<u>**May 2015**</u>
(some time after seeing David Tipper for the first couple times)

Words don't do life justice, and yet we speak.
I come to this high point of sensation
and lose touch with vocabulary.
To this point of unguarded understanding.
Oneness to the point where it just all makes too much sense for words...

I've just had a lot of thought-provoking life experience.

. . .

<u>**23 June 2015 12:05am**</u>

Somewhere in the air may lie an answer...

No matter how much I breathe
I can't figure it out.

Is it poison in this oxygen?

What could bring you closer to love?

Ask the right questions...

Where is the love?

Somewhere in the air my heart breaks all over again.

(Reading 'Night' by Elie Wiesel)
. . .

6 June 2011 1:45p
mskcc

<u>**4 Sept 2015**</u>
(28 years old)

Using pain to overcome it. Embracing the darkness as to let it become a part of me. Just a part of me and not all of me. We all hold that darkness within us, it's up to us as to what type of control it has.

. . .

Dusting off The Mirror

Context: My move to California set me on a mission of self-development without the influence of those who thought they knew me. Family may not mean to, but they put you in a box of their expectations. Giving you labels and ways of being. Separating yourself from this can help you find what it is *you* really like and want in your life. It was a beautiful start to something. I started dating a boy 4 years younger than me and he introduced me to so many new things and people to add to my life and growth.

Coping with my father's death had been difficult and beautiful in a lot of ways. Gratitude kept me going. And at the end of 2015, when I was about to approach 5 years without him, my mother had a massive hemorrhagic stroke 2 days before Christmas. Putting her in a coma that she would never come out of... We had to make the decision to let her go and remove the respirator that was keeping her alive... and on the evening of December 27th, 2015 with my loving sister by her side, my mother joined those before her and left this plane.

In the time period of 2016 to present 2020 I have done much introspection and reading on psychology and human development and potential. Blossoming into the bizarre human creature my parents set me out to be. I miss them every day. They are with me every day. I will not forget. I will never forget.

23 January 2016
(28 years old Santa Cruz, CA)

It seems as though, sometimes, PMS can feel like insanity when accompanied by heavy stress or grief... I can't handle much of anything right now... At points I can't stand my boyfriend... It's so scary... Am I gonna watch my life fall apart like the lives I've seen? Am I going to break under all this pressure?

I'm losing patience with everything. I feel as though I am harshest on [my boyfriend]... He's around me the most and I just want him to know what to do... I just want him to know how to comfort me... I just want him to fit in this box that I've made... God it breaks my heart... I think I might be crazy just because I am filled with so much love. An abundance of energy in a sick world

. . .

(Later the same day)

I sometimes daydream about killing myself...
not that I think I'd ever actually do it,
but I think the change of focus can be beneficial.
Momento Mori

My mother died
Lea Maria Charron 8.14.65 – 12.27.15
four years after my father
Jeffrey Donald Charron 9.25.63 – 11.5.11

I am currently, I think, the largest mess I have ever been in my short 28 years. PMS on top of all of this pain.

"Here, here's some pain and stress!
"Oh, wait, let me frost that with a hefty amount of hormones,
 So, you can be sure to irrationally deal with anything else that comes your way! You're welcome!"
Fuck.
    Fuck.
        Fuck.

Thought about hurting myself today...
It's been a while.
A long while.

. . .

<u>**3 March 2016**</u>
*(A piece written after my mother died suddenly and I went on a
life altering trip, in February, to Costa Rica)*

At the core of my being is the deepest sorrow. I feel as though
sadness and happiness are so close to being like the same thing.
I feel sad for every sorrowful feeling everyone ever has, but I
am so happy for their experience. All the pain I've ever felt
brought me to such a calm place. Though it's not always calm
there. Kind of like an ocean, it can be unruly. But in that feeling
lies some sense of reassurance.
I'm ALIVE.

Why must I feel so deeply? It is such a blessing and a curse. I
want to kiss away the tears of the world, but I also want them to
fall on their asses. I want them to find grace through struggle
and pain. Wake up to sensation and embrace it wholeheartedly.
Don't be afraid to feel and explore your own emotions.

If I don't give everything I have to give, I'll wallow away in
sadness. It's the only thing that makes sense in a world so full of
distraction and misdirection.

I just want to love the best way I can and help people to feel it.

Sometimes I get lost in it all.
My mind falls weak under all the weight
and fear seeps in again...
All in practice.
All in balance.
All in patience.

I thought after this trip I would feel readjusted. Maybe I do, but
it's just brought me a little closer to sorrow.

My mother is dead.
My father is dead.
I feel such a connection to it all.
Pain is very exhausting.

I feel so much. For everyone and everything.
Existence.
I wonder what I will bring to this life. <3

. . .

Saturday April 9th 2016 3:08am
(Santa Cruz, CA. 28 years old.
Almost 4 months after my mother passed)

I'm not even sure what's going on in my head these days. I feel as though I am making so much progress and then I feel like I'm thinking too much, and I just try to focus on nothing... It's Dazey. But something is happening. I'm growing immensely... This change is wild. It's both like a sandstorm and very calm. It makes me feel like I'm on the verge of tears a lot of times. But it feels good. It's not low. It's like... knowing. I think I am starting to feel so at one more often. The reminders and the practice are definitely starting to work. I feel calm in all of this madness.

I wonder what I will do with this gift.

. . .

<u>**30 April 2016**</u>

I am human...
You may find that a trivial fact,
but there is so much more to it than that.
CREATURE
Living breathing creature.
Surviving on a nervous, insecure, confidence
and it's beautiful. I am flawed. I am aware.
I have been known to be capable of mild douche-bagery.
I acknowledge, change, and move forward.
We all hope to not make the same mistakes...

Working forward, not backward
and not standing in place!
The road is wide open!
As are my eyes and mind.
I couldn't possibly be happier to be alive!
To breathe!
Things always look up when you look up,
but you won't learn that until you've looked down.
I'm looking up.
So should you.
The beauty in being human is too much
for me to comprehend.

. . .

30 April 2016

Let go of wondering
whilst giving into wonder.
It's all about balance.
Fluidly leave imprints on the ground.
Peace in myself will calm my perception of the world
around me...
I've merely chipped a piece off of an iceberg.

. . .

2 May 2016

Life is the path to death.
Don't just survive on the road to dying.
LIVE.
It's all about the journey, not the destination.
Live, laugh, and love this life you are living.

. . .

12 May 2016

If you care, you will always carry weight in your heart. Get to
know that weight. Invite it in. Show it around. Carry it with you
on your journeys and speak of it freely. We all have our own.

Embrace your sorrow... It is when your sorrow becomes so very
much a part of you, that your happiness has the opportunity to
truly blossom.

. . .

<u>**6 August 2016**</u>

As the waters roll by, I do my best to flow with the current...
Bouncing off rocks and scraping my knees,
I try to smile as these tears fall.
This heart will not be stopped by an inability to cope.
I will march on through this illusory reality with my wits about
me.
Ever changing, forever adapting.

. . .

<u>**19 August 2016**</u>
(29 years old)

If you believe in love. If you desire affection and kindness and maybe you're not receiving it... I suggest you GIVE it.
Screw how you currently feel and how those around you may be treating you... Stand up and love. Show them it doesn't matter how one feels or how one has been treated. No one has to treat others poorly merely because they FEEL poorly.
Merely because you've had a bad day at work. The act of giving love and making someone smile has the power of overcoming any sorrow or pain you may feel.
You feel poorly? Give love.
Angry? Give love.
Neglected? GIVE LOVE.
The better the example you set of how you think people should be treated, the better the treatment that comes back to you.

. . .

<u>12 September 2016</u>

At the edge of this current point of consciousness... Reaching... Feels more like falling down the steps... but it's brighter, so maybe I'm falling UP the steps. Feel like I'm always waiting for the gears to click into place. Once they click, they find there's a better place to be. Forever turning, adjusting... Adapting to surroundings while trying to be so patient with myself. It's friggin hard. It's harder to be patient with myself than it is to actually adapt... So strange. I wish this country didn't work so hard to strip us of our curiosities and beat us down into the only insecure creatures on the planet. Pushing forward trying not to think much. I find I often back myself into a corner thinking too much. Then I realize I merely need to flow more and focus on what makes me smile. It's that simple most times. Chasing smiles. Tomorrow should be good. ♡

. . .

<u>5 October 2016</u>

When we care about one another, everything falls into place... like magic.

. . .

<u>**30 November 2016**</u>

I am nothing but what I give to this world.
I am not what I say or what you say. I am what I do.
'I am' is being.
I need to constantly remind myself that I am forever growing.
It's important to remember that I will always be able to find
reasons to disagree with yesterday.
Whether it be with myself or not, it's never a good reason to take
away from today.
Forward Movements.
Always rearranging the walls in my mind.
Adapt or fall.

I invite into my life positive growth and change, as I walk through
it with love and light to share.

. . .

<u>**23 April 2017**</u>

I'm worried about you.
I'm worried about a society run by fear.
I'm concerned for the love that we all embody.
For our love that was manipulated and guided into fear.
Without knowing.

Why does it have to be so hard to open up
to love once we have been misled?
Has the damage been done so deep that it is irreparable?

Is it so hard to bring us back to our joyful state of life like we were as children? Before we were misled by an unwell society with mixed up priorities. When we knew the joy of life. The feeling of gratitude for just being able to exist and feel affection.

Somewhere we got lost, didn't we? Somehow, we were misled, and somehow that joy wasn't nurtured. Do you remember being happy as a child? And how it morphed and changed as ideas were put into our heads? As we were told we had to grow to fit into some idea someone else had for us... As we were told to compare ourselves to one another to force that growth. Being led to build ideas of what we should be like. Learning that it's acceptable to judge people and people don't change...

We've only done this for lack of a better idea. We've become complacent in this discomfort because it is how it has developed over generations. Well, as this society moves forward, we're seeing an incredible rise in mental illness. Can we not see that something is wrong? Nowadays it is not so uncommon for people to rely heavily on some sort of substance to try and manage their emotional discomfort. If not some illegal drug, often times our people cling to legal substances that seem to alleviate this discomfort... but to what end? Generations of uneasy bandages. Medicating a symptom of a much bigger problem. We need to get to the root of the problem. We need to stop the discomfort before it has an opportunity to develop.

How do you want to help?

. . .

<u>**12 August 2017**</u>
(30 years old. 2 days before my mother's birthday)

"Can you dress death up to hide it?" she said and threw my mind all over. Maybe it was mental illness, maybe it was drugs... Maybe it was the commonality of the two. but, either way, that one hit me hard. My lack of fear about dying makes me aware that it is life I'm actually afraid of... These steps it takes to grow. The strength it takes to persevere and continue to be happy... I know that death is freedom from these things. From these choices and obligations... Silly. Why does it have to be so difficult to be conscious? (Hahahaha) and maybe it doesn't have to be. Maybe we've just made it harder for ourselves... All this endless knowledge interfering with intuition and heart.

"Boredom's not a burden anyone should bear. Constant overstimulation numbs me." – Tool – Stinkfist

Getting to the root of thought by not thinking...?

Revert back to a toddler's state of mentality so there is possibility of true experience, free of judgement.
Innocent.

. . .

<u>**21 August 2017**</u>

a solar eclipse made my heart and brain do flips.
Smitten with existence and a question marked man.
A soul healing kick in the ass.
This shift has brought about a foot that wants to step on the gas.
Excitement fills my being.
4.3.2.1 and float. Go? Go floating.
The stars never let me down.
They surface me when I feel as though I'm drowning.
Here we go again, constantly shoving myself forward.

. . .

<u>**27 August 2017**</u>
(*30 years old*)

No use in questioning the flow, just go.

. . .

<u>**28 August 2017**</u>

I've learned how to slow down time by looking each moment in the eye. Bonding with existence makes an oxytocin high. Building a life raft out of brain chemicals. There are days when the raft can't hold up against the rapids of this life's path, smashing it into oblivion. And to the pieces I try to cling as I'm rushed by life's next opportunities...

New techniques. New rafts. New rapids to navigate. We rebuild and break again and again. The beauty of this flow too magnificent to allow it to dampen my spirits for long.

When exhaustion sets in you may cling onto something in this flow. Hoping you'll get some sort of break while you try and pause the go... all the while you're not noticing it's more tiring to fight the flow than to let go. Choking on waves and not allowing the growth that comes from all the smashing and the breaking... Amazing how this brilliant brain gets in the way of the massive magnitude of heart ability. Heart knows the flow. Heart has been in tune with the flow since before brain could even process it. Reconnecting with the heart-mind strange loop effect. Give and take. A constant exchange. Creation and creator.

. . .

30 August 2017

I'm just trying to enjoy the last bits of who I am today.
Tomorrow is another day.

In this ever changing being I am, I place my love.

Unmoved.
At the base of all that is changing that love stays the same. It just becomes more prominent and more developed. It's just a tiny piece of the universe stored inside of a shifting vessel. Every day I come to realize a little more how beautiful that is. How beautiful it is to be human. How blessed I am to be here in this experience. How strange! How elaborate!

I feel like I'm looking for my soul family... Maybe I have some of them but they are just far away from me... I wonder what is next for me on this journey. I leave for India in like 2 months and 2 weeks... My life is going to be so different.

<u>**Living Human Prism**</u>

A tiny piece of the universe stored inside a shifting vessel.
This vessel is decorated with the most vibrant colors, but there
is no light to see them.
it's because the light comes from within.
With a translucent vessel the light can make more colors than
one could even imagine.
You cannot get the light within if you do not first send it out.
Tear down your decorations to let the light shine through

. . .

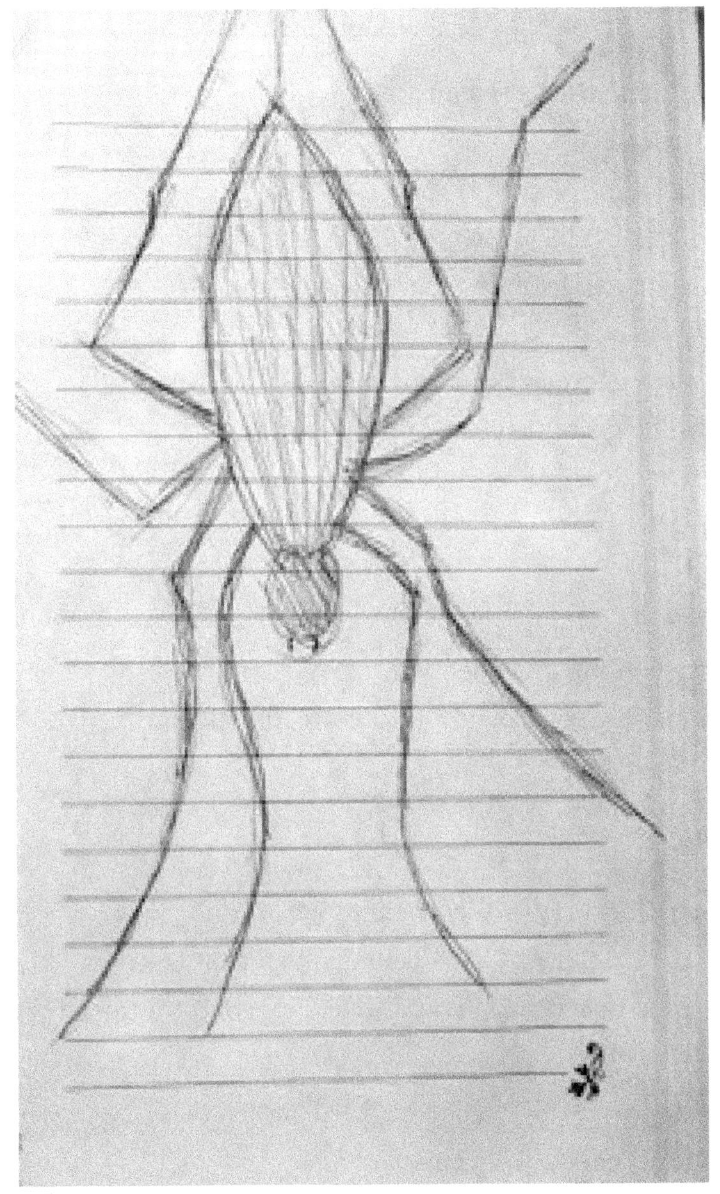

<u>**11 September 2017**</u>

It all seems so never ending..
but it does
it all does.

So, let go. Just let go.

These things around you are but things
it's the things inside you that give you wings

so let go

don't choke it till its end
and try to bring it to your own
silly thinking you can turn your coffin into throne.

. . .

Where am I? When is it?
I'm suddenly feeling like time is not.
Like what I once thought was water being thrown from a bucket
is now just…
a bucket.

No past. no future. just now.

A still life of ages.

And what to do with this now? Where to go?
Time to ask the heart some questions...

And what do you do with the blank stare reply?

Well, that's when brain chimes in all provocative,
Are you ready for some change?

. . .

Today would be my father's 54th birthday. Almost 6 years without him now. Isn't it amazing how the time flies? 6 years feels both like yesterday and 20 years ago.

Then in 3 months it will be a full 2 years without my mother, who would've turned 52 in August... November will be a full 6 years without my father.

I miss them so much. I'm very grateful to have pushed my life into a direction that is good for my heart and mind. Moving to California after my father died. He would've been so upset if I moved while he was alive... I understand why. I missed out on a lot of the last days of my mother's life due to this move.
Luckily, I'd go visit and had spent some good time with her about 6 months before she passed suddenly. I'm so grateful for the connection I shared with my parents. The love. The honesty. We told each other most everything... They helped me to see them as the humans they were and not the 'superhero parent' idea that children grow up with. Seeing my parents as the flawed and loving human beings they were really helped me develop into my own. It helped me to love them and become their friend.

Parents set you up with the perfect opportunities to learn. They help you to see characteristics you love and characteristics you don't love. All aiding in your development...
Pointing fingers at your parents for the things done wrong or not done right only hurts YOU. If you feel like pointing fingers it should be to say 'Hey, thanks for showing me what NOT to do.' They're all lessons. If you do not see this and adapt this way, you carry more pain than is truly necessary for forward growth... and you may not move forward at all.

I'm 30 years old. I'm single. My parents are deceased. I'm moving out of my amazing home in Santa Cruz California and going to India for 3.5 months. Unsure where I will land upon returning to the states. Possibly Colorado?

Life can be so up in the air. It's both exciting and a bit nerve wracking. I'm not afraid at least. I'm excited. These moments fly by but I'm learning how to truly enjoy each one. I am so grateful for this life's path. For the people in it. For the love I carry. I'm so grateful I have parents to miss. That they filled me so full it hurts that they're gone. So truly blessed.

Your perspective will save or take your life. You get to choose the angle from which to view your life. There is always a better angle.

I'm ready to put this heart and mind to the test. I'm ready to be brought to new stages of exhaustion and understanding. I'm ready for growth. Ready for this next life shift.
Excited.

I am the most sorrowful I have ever been in my life... and I have never been more contented. I've come to a beautiful understanding of life and struggle. An understanding that frees me of so much.
There are no words for this feeling. Any and all cheapen its pulse...
I can only tell you it's like the golden sunshine that pours in my window... It's calm. It's powerful.
It's love.

Today the calm sorrow is very present. A calm sorrow littered with appreciation. So much gratitude for this path.

Happy 54th Birthday Dad.
Thank you. I love you.

Jeffrey Charron- September 25th 1963 - November 5th 2011
Lea Charron - August 14th 1965 - December 27th 2015

Two incredible life paths that affected so many others.
So, blessed to be born of this connection.

Be grateful for your interactions. Find purpose within them. Whether positive or negative every interaction has something to teach us. Maybe it will teach us about the world. About human nature. About emotion itself. Maybe it has something to teach you about YOU. I've had some really difficult interactions in the past 2 years... Interactions that brought me to new levels of emotion... Places of severe emotional discomfort. These difficult communications could have very well kept my mind within negative boundaries. but when you have a negative mindset your life tends to follow suit. Luckily, I had the opportunity to learn this earlier on and I knew I had to find a way out of this victimized mind state.

I've managed to alter my perspective in a manner that saves my relationships and my heart and mind. It is not easy, but it does become easier. With this perspective shift I am able to see what is at the core of human emotional outbursts. Pain. Discomfort.

"The way people treat you speaks about who they are, not about you" or something like that. This is true. Projection is a very real thing. You can see this yourself when you find yourself out bursting about something. You can get to the bottom of it and find what it is about yourself that made you act in such a manner. I've done it. I still do it. And in keeping in this practice of acknowledgment I can adjust my behavior accordingly. I am much calmer these days as I practice understanding. I am working so hard emotionally to develop and nurture this love that is my being. This love that I believe we are all born of. I can always do better. I can always love better. I strive for this continued growth... We are all hurting. We all struggle... I hope you believe me when I say I love you... because it's true. I love you at the core of your human existence. I love the child in your heart. I love your wounds. I love the love that I know resides within us all and I hope to help wake it up. I'm pushing out what I'm hoping for in this world. In this life... Connection. Love.

Understanding. Appreciation. Gratitude... and I'll tell you, it comes back to you in the most beautiful ways. It also brings you to new and difficult places of struggle. There will always be struggle no matter the path you choose. Choose a brighter path and you will be better able to handle the discomfort they have to offer you... I say offer because discomfort is an opportunity. Discomfort is an opportunity to practice what you have learned in your life. It's an opportunity to adapt...

I invite into my life positive growth and change, as I walk through it with love and light to share. Positive growth and change can often stem from feeling discomfort.

I strive to handle my difficulties with grace, and I know I will always fall a little short, but this will not stop my process. I strive to always be humble enough to admit my mistakes. I hope to always have enough courage to apologize when apologies are due, and the gratitude and understanding to accept the faults and flaws of others in this unbelievably odd existence we share. If you give the love, it will be returned.

. . .

<u>**6 November 2017**</u>
(6 years after my father died, also his mother's birthday)

Sometimes life changes on you,
sometimes you have to change on it.
An equal teeter totter.
Balance.
Give into the flow and, the flow will give into you.

High on existence.

Letting love shape my reality.

The love that I embody is an extension of the universe.
An incredible adaptive energy flowing through a shape shifting vessel

Taking steps towards a grave so full.

. . .

<u>**28 December 2017**</u>
(Goa, *India. 2 years after my mom died,
also, her father's birthday)*

Let your gratitude guide you to your grave.

. . .

<u>January 2018</u>
(Bankikodla, India)

"I don't like the way my honesty looks on other people's faces"
a young BK

Being honest saves so much suffering
and creates so much growth.
The worst thing that can happen is you don't like the outcome of
your honesty, but it sets things in motion. In the direction of truth.
The way things flow. The way they're meant to flow.
Speak your truth.
Out of necessity for forward growth. Not with insensitivity, but
with an intent to find and keep your path clear of things that no
longer grow you and serve you well.

. . .

<u>January 2018</u>
(Shankar Prasad Ashram, Bankikodla, India)

*Something I wrote after a profound Yoga Nidra experience
(sleep meditation), with focus on the Muladhara Chakra
(Root Chakra)*

I found my parents on a hill...
by a rose filled with the universe...

They held my hands and reminded me that I am love.

They are with me always.

I feel as though that hill is always there.
That they're there watching me and sending me their love.
I can always find them there...

As we look down onto the city
I remember I'm not afraid.

'I will love myself unconditionally.'

Everyone is me and I am everyone.
I am my parents.
And we are all love.

I saw my mother in a river and a deer walked away. I cast my
bag into the river and carried on up the hill to be reminded of
the light that is my soul.

I fall back into my gratitude.
My home.
My life.
Home sweet gratitude.

I will remember that I am love.
I will help spread this light throughout the world.

Breathing into the connection.
I love you.

. . .

<u>**6 February 2018**</u>
(Auroville, India)

If we all pointed fingers at, judged, and/or removed ourselves from every person, for every misguided, unjustified, inappropriate, unkind thing they did, there would be no connection left in the world.
Try to see people for the wounded, love seeking creatures they are. Only love can heal these wounds. If you ever feel the need to judge someone, first take a look in the mirror.

(Later the same day)

The universe will provide you with the experiences that are appropriate for your stage of growth. It is up to you to acknowledge them and use them to think, see, and do things differently.
Keeping in a positive mindset.

. . .

<u>**11 February 2018**</u>
(Auroville, India)
Feeling like the universe

This ever-changing flow can make me so dizzy... Whirlwinded. Climbing to the tippity top of my consciousness. Connecting with the divine...
Sometimes it's full-on source connection. Most times it's just glimpses and reminders... Getting just a peak at what I once felt... Then I lose grip and start falling... Thankfully I've built this gratitude trampoline that catapults my ass back up to a firm grip and a steady climb.

Just keep trying. Just keep bouncing back. Keep remembering.

Learning is remembering and what you are is in the doing. Remember and DO. Do not punish yourself for slipping. Punishing yourself nails your foot to the floor. Build a trampoline of reminders and GET BACK UP. You are love. You are a bad mf'n ass. You are HUMAN. YOU ARE THE MF'N UNIVERSE.

 The milky way is not concerned that it's being sucked into a supermassive black hole. It just keeps spiraling. Be the universe you are. With all its divinity and nothingness.

This amazing balance of knowing you are nothing and everything at the same time. Try to find comfort in that. Otherwise...
What's this heart even beating for?
YOU ARE LOVE. Don't be afraid.

LET GO.

I will love myself unconditionally, and I will spread that love throughout the world.
'Be the light that shines through'

. . .

<u>9 March 2018</u>
(Napa or Ukiah, California)

I am some strange humany manifestation of love... It seems like some kind of oxymoron these days but it's true. I am love that came in the form of ignorance.
Isn't that weird?
I am love that is stuck in an emotionally suppressed container...
Life's like 'Ha! Good luck figuring this one out fucker!'

<u>20 March 2018</u>

I want positivity in my life, so I invite it in with positivity.
You don't invite a friend into your home with bitterness, this
will cause your friend to be bitter as well. You open your door
with love and compassion, and it all falls into place.

. . .

<u>25 May 2018</u>
(Coulterville, CA)

Where your focus goes, so goes your life.
Direct your focus.

. . .

<u>30 June 2018</u>

Nurture your toddle heart...
This is the secret to lessening suffering.

. . .

<u>3 July 2018</u>
(Day after my 31ˢᵗ birthday)

Sometimes life changes on you...
Sometimes you gotta change on it...

. . .

<u>**4 August 2018**</u>

Words like these steps I'm afraid to take...
Afraid to say...
Afraid to live.
Be. Do.

Harness the epic badassery that is unconditional love.
Vibrate.
Let the world know this
Truth.
Breathing into the connection
Like a deep stretch in your heart that reaches your mind.
Don't let go of that loop.
Meditate on the flow of brain to heart and back again,
so as not to forget but learn through remembering.
Trying to fall back into the flow by letting go.
Again, and again and again.

. . .

<u>**30 August 2018**</u>

"Each day, in itself, brings with it an eternity."
- Paulo Coelho - The Alchemist

I know you're terrified of achieving your dreams.
Horrified you're actually capable of doing big things.

Worried you won't be able to fill imaginary shoes.

Well, you're only as brilliant as you allow yourself to shine.

What are you afraid of?
Being a better person than you were
yesterday?
Growing? Striving? Believing? Achieving?
Replace this fear with love and your problem is solved.
Love for yourself. Love for those around you.
By setting a good example of working towards our dreams.

"The joy in life is to be used for a purpose. I want to be used up
when I die." - George Bernard Shaw

This journey is short, but it's long than it seems. So really make
it count and try to reach your dreams.

. . .

10 September 2018
(Groveland, CA)

I invite into my life positive growth and change, as I walk through
it with love and light to share.

A loving overflow. Spilling over the edges of this glass so full.
Still learning to comfortably embrace this solitude. Being there
for you is the most important thing you can learn to do.
In a life based around interaction, learn how to interact with
yourself.

Discover your capacity for self-love, appreciation, and
entertainment. Your heart and mind do love you, love them back.

. . .

<u>**11 November 2018**</u>
(Columbia, CA. 7 years after dad died)

See God within everyone.
How would you treat God if you were before He/She/It? God lives within everyone you know. Everyone you don't know. It's easier to see the differences on the surface then to see the light within... To see God within. This is the meaning of Namaste. God in me sees God in you, and in this place, we are one.

I find the best way to find the light when it can be difficult, is to see everyone around us like the toddlers they started out as... and the infant before that. These young humans left behind in search of 'adulthood'. We are all still these toddlers... Pained and yearning for affection and acceptance. See that heart and love it. This alone can heal the world.

* * *

I pray for understanding in the hearts and minds of all humans... and for the continued blossoming of that love in the ones who are already there.

. . .

<u>**2 December 2018**</u>

Honesty is the key to happiness, and the beginning of self-love.

. . .

<u>20 December 2018</u>
(Columbia, CA)

I remember once saying that I was 'In love with the world... not how it is, but how it could be.'
After all these years... After all these mental shifts from growing through experience. I now realize I am in love with the world exactly how it is. That in this madness is it's perfection. That is, there is beauty in this undeniable dissonance. Without this disharmony there would be no rise and without rise there would be nowhere to fall from... Necessary ebbs and flows of creation and destruction. Peace in chaos.
Like tears from laughter and laughter from sadness. Embracing this existence in its entirety and playing the part you're meant to play. That means not just sitting in resignation with the tragedy in the world merely because you acknowledge its importance... It is a FLOW. Don't just be a wall... A dam... Damn.
We have this unbelievably odd opportunity to affect our surroundings... our ability to survive depends solely on our ability to interact with our environment and enhancing this ability is not only something we're capable of but it is necessity as humankind... A necessity for future human survival is enhancing our ability to interact with our environment. Which doesn't mean inventing more tools with which to do so... It means harnessing the tools with which we were born and mastering them. All of these worldly, cultural distractions keeping us all from connecting to one another... Fighting against the vibration that unites us all. Wedging fear in between our mind and heart connection to keep us away from the power that rises from it.

DON'T BE AFRAID. Dissolve the boundaries.
CONNECT.
LOVE. LOVE. LOVE. (say it louder for the people in the back!)

LOVE!! PEOPLE!! LOVE!!

This is how to enhance your ability. This is the key to opening
every locked door. Mold your key. Carve it. Wield it.
AND GIVE IT AWAY FREELY.

This is where the rise comes in. This blabbering is part of it...
You're part of it. Every moment an opportunity to grow and add.
A being of such emotional growth does not merely navigate this
world with legs and mind... this is a heartfelt journey. Put your
mind beneath your feet and use your heart to lead the way.
This way, we rise.
Feel it. I know you do.

. . .

79

<u>**6 January 2019**</u>

They're all tests. Every interaction is a pop quiz. How will you use what you've learned to handle your changing situations? Running mind through heart is usually the best option... Unless you about to die, ya know, then hop on that fight or flight life... but don't live there, yea? That shits not comfortable. Life shouldn't be about mere survival, it's about thriving. Bob and weave with this flow of obstacles. A lighthearted calmness can save us from so much struggling... Foresight. Look down the paths of potentiality and accept all fates. This can help bring about the calmness that helps the flow. Keeps the go. Life is bloody magnificent people. It's insane. That lonesome feeling and I play on a teeter totter. A zoom in zoom out balance. Sometimes you need to overindulge in the zoom... freak yourself out a bit... all part of the process. No mistakes ya know? You know.

Haven't written in a while. I'm liking the blabber flow this Sunday morning. There's this place inside of all of us that carries a potential for a sense of immense freedom. Under any and all circumstances... have you touched it? Have you felt it? If you have then I don't have to explain.
Glimpses. Like trying to squeeze through a door that's only cracked open... but you can't force it... it will open more when we're ready... I think... just keep getting glimpses and feelings through that crack... but when we're ready there's no other option but to walk through into that freedom.

Ego has this amazing ability to beat you into shape. It's interesting. Another odd necessity. It creates so many issues for us, yet it can also inspire us to make changes in our lives to fit into the seemingly unrealistic shoes it's created for us. As long as we can be honest with ourselves, ego can be useful, and until it is no longer needed it harasses us... hm. That's an interesting idea... There's a purpose to all of it. The energy cycling around works in mysterious and magical ways. Impressive. A bit confusing... but what's there to get? Why? Why always ask why? That their brain gets in the way of the flow ya know?... ha.

Guess I'll shut up now, was a fun brain spew.

. . .

20 May 2019
(Columbia, CA. 31 years old
5 days after my head on collision- Not at fault)

Heaven is the result of healing yourself by understanding and
loving the process of existence...
You create heaven when you have fully arrived in hell.

The only way out of the suffering of 'Yin' is to love it.
Arrive.
When you feed fear with love it is satiated.
This was the meal it wanted all along.

<u>8 July 2019</u>
(32 years old, Sonora, CA)

Using God to make life insignificant.
Normalizing blessings to praise insecurities over lessons...
One clumsy foot in front of the other.

Crying, complaining, and clinging to a band-aid while we injure
ourselves beneath its cotton.
Adhered to our emotional output.
There is no clot if you don't bleed...

The healing is IN the feeling.

. . .

<u>15 July 2019</u>

The monster inside directed at you.
An ego dance where the darkness spins around itself...
An argument.
The tornado that feeds itself
Two faces turned away from knowing...

Too hostile for positivity.

They say opposites attract.
Well, not when it comes to how you act.

Drowning in flames wondering how you ever held water to begin
with...
"It'll take a lot to put this out..." you mumble with your hands off
the wheel.

Feels like falling... but it's merely an opportunity for flight.
A chance to shape-shift.
Transmutate.
Evolve and communicate.

<u>**16 July 2019**</u>
(Sonora, CA)

Born with the ability to question intention... Question instinct.

Born with the potential for choice...

To be a douche bag?
Or be a voice?

On the brink of new words.
New worlds.

If I touched your heart would you feel it?
Did you even know you had a heart to touch?
That needs to be touched.

Separation from self.
Touch yourself.

Free will?
Loose will.
Needs tightening.
Fine tuning.

Choking on the emotions lodged in our throats.
A pharmaceutical dam.
Damn.

Is this what God was looking for?
Do you see him smiling down on you while you watch the evening news?

Wide eyed and amazed at what his children do?

It's time for a shift in the paradigm mind.

Why are we holding our breath?
God can be found between the inhale and the exhale
but you will not find him by choking on air...

. . .

<u>26 October 2019</u>
(Columbia, CA)

Can you support yourself?
Will you?
Believe.
It is your 'we' that will save you.
It's all inside. Freedom lies within.
Have faith and trust the energetic process
Direct your energy to what it is you want to see

You are love. You're not done yet. You are needed. Heal.
You are valued. HEAL. You have purpose.
Help someone.

We are born of the slow death of a galaxy
From this we have
Love/Fear
      Life/Death
           Yang/Yin

From this we have
Confusion
a constant spinning and twirling of thought
Ka is a wheel

Existing as the slow death of the milky way
A divine miracle of somewhat organized chaos.

Miscellaneous
Undated Writings
(2017-2019)

<u>The Patient</u>

Sometimes I miss you with all my heart.
Then I remember why we're apart.

It never stopped me from loving you
Always, through and through

Your broken heart so easy to hold
with this bleeding heart of mine, so I'm told...

It'll wear me down if I don't keep my head
This heart of mine so easily lead

through the doors to a passionate space
where it's hard for head to keep up the pace

I must be cautious in a world so crass
To put on the brakes could probably save my ass.

So here I walk without distress
your heart always beating within my chest

That loving shine will stay forever
no matter, whatever... not afraid of the weather

and now these calm, slow, patient steps
will guide me to loves sweet caress.

Phantom Comfort

We always ask 'Why?'...
It was this fruit of knowledge that brought about the world's
biggest lie.

A fear of ignorance
        built from a throne behind our biggest fence

The answer to 'Why?' is...
        'because   you   don't   need   to   know.'
because how far will you let that go?
To the point where the mind can't seem to feel.
To complete distraction from our need to heal.

A certain ignorance can give blissfully to intuition
A balance of mind and heart that can keep one incredibly gifted

. . .

Bumping into insecurities
unruly sea without much ease.
WHO THE FUCK ARE YOU SUPPOSED TO PLEASE?!
It's where we listen from,
That's the hand with the smoking gun.
You're in the driver's seat
Need to make heart and mind meet.

Mind tells heart to be cool,
Heart tells mind 'Don't act a fool'

Then the words pour in like objective soup
Helps solidify the heart-mind loop
bringing peace to our next stage
It's time for humanity to act it's age

. . . .

<u>Untitled/Undated</u>
<u>Short Ramblings</u>
(2019)

Stuck inside your own head?
Who elses head could you be stuck in?
Should you be stuck in?
Stop looking for a door
-: Exit does not exist :-
-Get Comfortable-
Reorganize
To see with your own eyes
That life is your prize.
It's about time to realize

. . . .

Inability to think clearly.
Muddled up with energy.
Need feet in dirt and head in the trees
It is my soul I'd like to please

-:Release:-
-:With Hold:-

Turning insides into gold

Internal alchemy to set you free

Let the inner buddha unfold

. . . .

What we've been up to while life was working
on adapting past fear

                    -: Distraction :-

Fear will not stop this forward moving heart
Step forward into growth

                    -:- TAO -:-

Storms are part of the way
Tempest littered Tao
The winds will move you
or move without you
Mountains crumble to will

                            . . . .

The energy in you chose to be here
It chose this life in this body
it chose this family and these struggles
It chose <u>you</u>

Remember
You are love. Don't be afraid.

<u>Afterword</u>
Direct the reflect

Thank you for taking the time to feel all this life with me. Approaching 33 is strange. It's the age my father was when he was diagnosed with cancer; I was 8. Time is a fascinating thing. Life doesn't seem to move if you don't let it... which gives time this odd perception of flying by... The more I've grown and healed, the more I've learned to *choose* life. Allow life. Slow it down. Offering up myself to the flow while mediating the communication between heart and mind, so the flow knows where to go.

If you're in a difficult place... Feel it. I don't want to tell you what you already know. 'This too shall pass' sometimes warrants a punch in the face ;) Because we know this and knowing things doesn't always help with the severity of emotion. What I do want you to know, what 'This too shall pass' really means, is you will only be this very version of you right now. Appreciate it like it's the last time you'll ever get to eat ice cream. I'll never be 32 again. There are always things to appreciate in our places of discomfort.

You are worth your patience. You are worth all the love. You are worth your tears and your feelings. If I can crawl out of an angry, confused, hole in the dark, to find the light and love, and still be confused, so can you :)

Life is amazing. Choose it.

And if you find yourself struggling so deeply you don't think you can choose life anymore, please reach up. I know it's hard and those dark days can feel like none of this is worth it... I promise you it is. This life is worth losing my parents. This experience is worth everything it brings. Sometimes we need to change our environment and create better experiences. We don't get to choose the circumstances our lives are born into, but we can choose what we do with them.

And yes, sometimes entire days need to be spent in bed. But get up tomorrow because it's a new day.

I invite into my life positive growth and change, as I walk through it with love and light to share.

Walk with me.

"Your need for acceptance will make you invisible in this world. Risk being seen in all of your glory."
-Jim Carrey

Special thanks to the man who spent 8 years actively doing the best he knew how to love me. I would not be who I am today without everything we went through together. I am grateful for all of it and always so sorry for where I fell short. C'est la vie.

I love you always. Thank you.

Questions or concerns about ideas written in here?
Feel free to send an email to AdaptToSurviveKat@gmail.com

Namaste my friends.

Hybrid Sequence Media Bibliography

001- Bring Something Dead
002- Meat Grinder
003- From the Belly of the Goat
004- Mr. Miyagi's Soggy Cereal
005- Separation: Healing
006- Rogue
007- Shrapnel
008- The Word For Poetry Is Poetry
009- Catacomb Kittens
0010- Bottomlands